# The White House

## Introducing Primary Sources

by Kathryn Clay

CAPSTONE PRESS
a capstone imprint

Little Explorer is published by Capstone Press,
1710 Roe Crest Drive, North Mankato, Minnesota 56003
www.mycapstone.com

**Library of Congress Cataloging-in-Publication Data**
Library of Congress Cataloging-in-Publication Data is available on the Library of Congress website.
ISBN 978-1-5157-6356-7 (library binding)
ISBN 978-1-5157-6361-1 (paperback)
ISBN 978-1-5157-6365-9 (eBook PDF)

**Editorial Credits**
Brenda Haugen, editor; Veronica Scott and Philippa Jenkins, designers; Kelli Lageson, media researcher; Tori Abraham, production specialist

Our very special thanks to Jim Barber, Historian, National Portrait Gallery, Smithsonian, for his curatorial review. Capstone would also like to thank the following at Smithsonian Enterprises: Kealy Gordon, Product Development Manager, Ellen Nanney, Licensing Manager, Brigid Ferraro, Vice President, Education and Consumer Products, Carol LeBlanc, Senior Vice President, Education and Consumer Products, and Christopher A. Liedel, President.

**Photo Credits**
We would like to thank the following for permission to reproduce photographs: Alamy/H.S. Photos, 20; Bridgeman Images: Peter Newark American Pictures, 11, UIG/Universal History Archive, 25, 29; Granger, NYC - All rights reserved, 8 (left and right), 13, 16, 19, 24, 28; Library of Congress: 6, 7, 9, 12, 14, 15, 21, 22, 23 (left and right), 26, 27; North Wind Picture Archives, 17; Shutterstock: PRANAV VORA, 4, Sean Pavone, cover

Printed in the United States of America.
102017    010872R

# Table of Contents

# Primary Sources

When an event happens, people often write about it in letters or diaries. They also take photographs and read about it in newspapers. These items are called primary sources. They help to paint a picture of past events.

a photograph of the White House

Primary sources also serve as evidence of a certain time or place. Building designs, paintings, and old maps are also primary sources. These things tell us the history of the White House.

## The White House at a Glance

- located at 1600 Pennsylvania Avenue, Washington, D.C.

- includes 132 rooms, 35 bathrooms, 412 doors, and 147 windows

- 570 gallons (2,158 liters) of paint are needed to cover the outside

- has been called President's Palace, the President's House, and the Executive Mansion

- first called the White House in 1901 by President Theodore Roosevelt

- has a tennis court, swimming pool, movie theater, and one-lane bowling alley

# Plans for a New Home

George Washington became the first president of the United States in 1789. The White House had not yet been built. Instead, Washington lived in New York City. Later he moved to Philadelphia, Pennsylvania.

an 1851 engraving on cream wove paper of George Washington by Christian Schussele

**FACT**

Maryland and Virginia donated land near the Potomac River for the capital city. Washington named the area District of Columbia after Christopher Columbus.

Washington thought the president needed a grand home. But he wasn't sure if the house should be in the North or the South. The Residence Act was passed on July 16. It allowed land near the Potomac River to become the nation's capital city. Later named Washington, D.C., this area was between the North and the South.

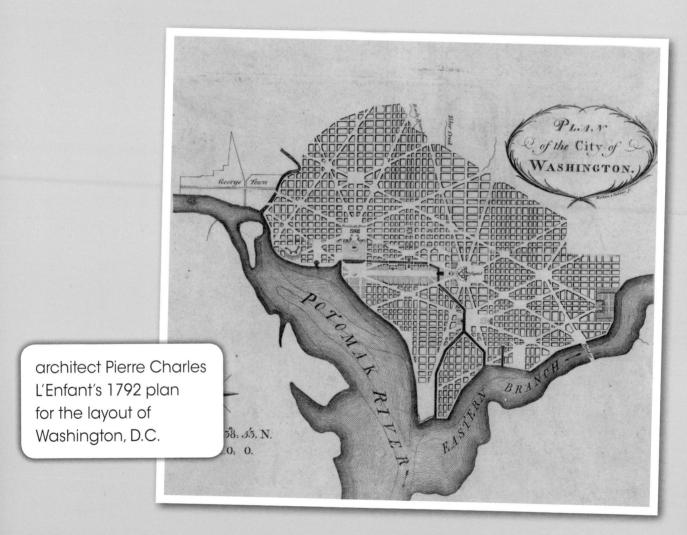

architect Pierre Charles L'Enfant's 1792 plan for the layout of Washington, D.C.

# Choosing a Design

Washington wanted the house to be a symbol of the presidency. It would be both a home and an office for the president. It also needed to be large enough to host visitors. But he did not want a palace.

Among the plans submitted for the White House were these from Thomas Jefferson (below) and James Diamond (right).

Secretary of State Thomas Jefferson held a contest to find a designer. Nine people shared their plans. The winning design came from architect James Hoban.

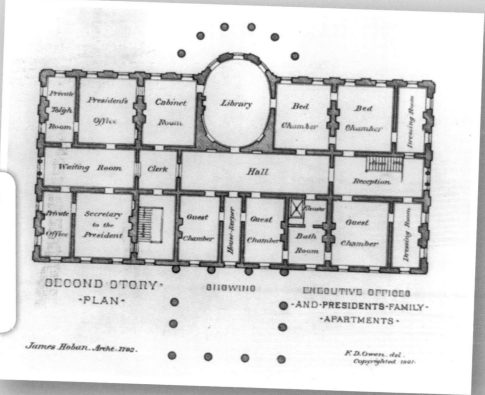

James Hoban's plan for the second story of the White House included offices, space for guests, and bedrooms.

## FACT

Prior to winning the contest, James Hoban had designed a bank, a courthouse, and several large homes. But the White House is his most famous design. Hoban also oversaw the building of the U.S. Capitol.

Washington laid the first stone on October 13, 1792. Sandstone was hauled in from Virginia. Workers covered the sandstone in a thick, white paint. The paint acted as a sealant and helped to keep the stones weather-tight.

Building continued for eight years. The total cost to build the White House was $232,372. When finished it was the largest home in the United States.

## FACT

Hoban's design for the White House was modeled on the first and second floors of Leinster House, a palace in Dublin, Ireland.

an 1800 engraving of the White House

# First Residents

The White House wasn't finished in time for George Washington to live there. President John Adams and his wife, Abigail, were the first residents. The couple moved in on November 1, 1800. But much of the building was unfinished. Only six rooms were completed. Like all houses at that time, there were no bathrooms or running water.

a portrait of Abigail Adams by Benjamin Blyth created around 1766

Abigail used a large, unfurnished room to hang laundry. She didn't think the president's clothes should be hung outside. This room later became the East Room.

# Presidential Privy

Running water wasn't available in the White House until 1833. The first modern toilet was added to the White House in the 1850s, when Millard Fillmore was president. President William Howard Taft, who weighed more than 300 pounds (136 kilograms), added a bathtub in 1908. The bathtub was large enough to fit four average-size adults.

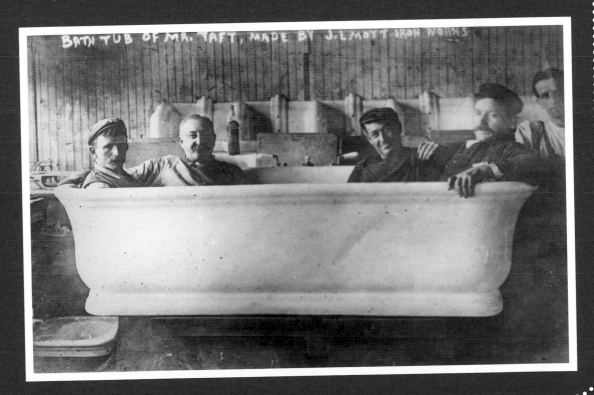

# Jefferson Moves In

Thomas Jefferson became president in 1801. His wife had died in 1782, and he thought the White House was too large for just himself. He thought about living somewhere else. But he moved in anyway and started to make changes.

a lithograph from around 1928 based on a painting of Thomas Jefferson by Gilbert Stuart

His first addition was a flushing toilet. He also added a drawing room and a small museum. Then Jefferson opened the White House to the public. Today the White House is still a popular place for tourists to visit.

**FACT**

Jefferson's daughter Patsy gave birth to a son during Jefferson's second term. The baby was the first child born in the White House.

# The British Burn It Down

During the War of 1812 (1812–1814), British soldiers marched through the capital city. On August 24, 1814, they set fire to the White House. President James Madison and his wife, Dolley, escaped. But the inside of the building was ruined.

an illustration by Joseph Boggs Beale of residents fleeing from Washington, D.C., as British soldiers set fires

An illustration by Gerry Embleton shows Dolley Madison saving the portrait of George Washington.

Hoban was asked to rebuild the White House. Using the original design and new materials, he finished the work in 1817. By then James Monroe was the new president. He was the first to live in the rebuilt White House.

# Executive Offices

President Theodore Roosevelt made many changes to the White House in 1902. He moved the president's offices to the west part of the main floor. This area is now known as the West Wing. Before the West Wing was added, these offices were located on the second floor along with the living spaces.

## Important Events in the Oval Office

- October 22, 1962: President John Kennedy's speech announcing the Cuban Missile Crisis

- August 8, 1974: President Richard Nixon resigns office

- January 28, 1986: President Ronald Reagan's speech following the Space Shuttle *Challenger* explosion

- September 11, 2001: President George W. Bush's speech following the terrorist attacks on the United States

President William Taft added the Oval Office in 1908. It has been the main office for every president since. The Oval Office got its name from its oval shape. Presidents have chosen their own decorations and furniture for the office.

the Oval Office as it looked in the 1970s when Richard Nixon was president

The White House needed major repairs by 1945. Walls and floors were falling apart. Some people even talked about tearing down the crumbling building.

a photograph of the White House repairs from around 1950

Harry Truman was president at the time. During the rebuilding, he stayed across the street at the Blair House. The Blair House is used as a guest house for presidential visitors.

a photograph of the Blair House from around 1918

Truman gave a televised tour of the renovated White House in 1952. He showed off the improvements that had been done. Workers made sure all the repairs matched the original design.

# The East Room

One of the most famous rooms in the White House is the East Room. The largest room in the White House, it has been used for concerts, receptions, and weddings. Five presidential daughters have been married in the East Room.

a photo of East Room of the White House from the first half of the 1900s

The rescued painting of George Washington now hangs in the East Room. The East Room is also where people came and mourned presidents Abraham Lincoln and John F. Kennedy after their assassinations.

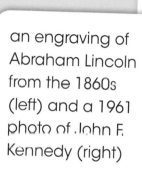

an engraving of Abraham Lincoln from the 1860s (left) and a 1961 photo of John F. Kennedy (right)

## FACT

Several of the first children used the East Room for roller skating. President Jimmy Carter's daughter, Amy, left marks from her skates. The marks remained until the floor was repaired 30 years later.

# Family Quarters

Presidents and their families live on the second floor of the White House. This floor has 16 rooms and six bathrooms. There's also a dining room and a kitchen.

a 1970 photograph of the Lincoln Bedroom, one of the most famous rooms in the White House

The third floor was used into the 1950s as staff bedrooms. But staff no longer live in the White House. Now the third floor has a game room and exercise room.

a 1902 photo of the updated kitchen in the White House

## FACT

When Bill Clinton was president (1993–2001), a music room was added to the third floor. Clinton played his saxophone in the soundproof room.

# The White House Today

People must make reservations several weeks before they visit the White House. When it is open for tours, about 6,000 people visit the White House in a day. Tourists see the East Room, the Red Room, and other public areas.

Children enjoy the Easter Egg Roll at the White House in 1914.

The White House also opens for special events. Twice each year the White House Gardens are open to the public. Visitors can walk through the Rose Garden. At Easter crowds gather for the Easter Egg Roll. Others come to see beautifully decorated Christmas trees during the holidays.

the official portrait of First Lady Michelle Obama in 2009 by photographer Joyce N. Boghosian

"The White House isn't simply a home to First Families or meeting space for world leaders, it's also known as 'The People's House,' a place that should be open to everyone ... Thousands of people have walked these halls and gazed at the artwork. They've examined the portraits of Washington, Lincoln, and Kennedy. They've imagined the history that's unfolded here. And now you can do all of that without leaving your home [because of the Internet]."

– Former First Lady Michelle Obama

## White House Safety

Keeping the president safe is an important job. The White House has many safety features in place. All of the windows are bulletproof. An iron gate surrounds the grounds. Guards are stationed at all of the entrances.

Secret Service agents follow the president everywhere. They are also located throughout the house and grounds. Members of the Secret Service are specially trained to protect the president.

# Timeline

**1792**    James Hoban is chosen to design the White House

**October 13, 1792**    White House construction begins

**November 1, 1800**    John and Abigail Adams move into the White House

**August 24, 1814**    British soldiers burn down the White House

a 1970 photograph of the State Dining Room at the White House

a 1950 photograph of construction equipment outside the White House during a major renovation

1817    rebuilding the White House is complete

1901    officially named the White House

1902    West Wing is added

1908    Oval Office is added

1948    workers begin major renovations to the White House

1952    renovations are finished

# Glossary

**architect**—a person who designs and draws plans for buildings, bridges, and other construction projects

**artifact**—an object used in the past that was made by people

**assassination**—the act of killing someone who is well known or important

**capital**—the city where a country's government meets and makes laws

**evidence**—information and facts that help prove something or make you believe that something is true or false

**executive**—a person with great responsibility

**primary source**—an original document

**reception**—a formal party

**renovate**—to restore something to good condition

**reservation**—a saved spot

**resident**—a person who lives someplace permanently

**resign**—to give up a job or position voluntarily

**symbol**—an object that reminds people of something else. The White House is a symbol of the presidency.

**tourist**—a person who is visiting a place for fun

# Read More

**Connors, Kathleen**. *What's It Like to Live in the White House?* White House Insiders. New York: Gareth Stevens Publishing, 2015.

**Ferguson, Melissa**. *American Symbols: What You Need to Know.* Fact Files. North Mankato, Minn: Capstone Press, 2017.

**Stine, Megan**. *Where Is the White House?* Where Is…? New York: Grosset & Dunlap, 2015.

**Wilson, Jon**. *The White House.* Mankato, Minn.: Childs World, 2014.

# Internet Sites

Use FactHound to find Internet sites related to this book.

Visit *www.facthound.com*

Just type in 9781515763567 and go.

 Check out projects, games and lots more at
**www.capstonekids.com**

# Critical Thinking Questions

1. The White House is a historical building. Think about the buildings in your town. Are any of them historic buildings?

2. Compare the White House designs on pages 8 and 9. How are they different? How are they the same?

3. How has the White House changed since it was first built?

# Index